Advent for children

Freya Jaffke

Advent
for children

Floris Books

Translated by Donald Maclean
Illustrated by Christiane Lesch

First published in German under the title
Advent, Anregungen für die Vorweihnachtszeit
by Verlag Freies Geistesleben, Stuttgart, 1979.
First published in English by Floris Books in 1983.

© 1979 Verlag Freies Geistesleben
GmbH Stuttgart

This translation © Floris Books, 1983

Reprinted 1986

British Library Cataloguing in Publication Data

Jaffke, Freya
Advent for children.
1. Church calendar — Juvenile literature
2. Advent — Juvenile literature
I. Title   II. Maclean, Donald
III. Advent.   English
263'.91   BV40

ISBN 0-86315-009-8

Printed in Great Britain
by John Bartholomew & Son Ltd, Edinburgh

Contents

Foreword

'When's my birthday?' 'When's Christmas?' These are the landmarks of the children's year. And what an immensity of waiting there is from one birthday, one Christmas to the next! The celebration of Advent, the four weeks preceding Christmas, draws together and focuses this longing and expectancy.

The surroundings have a strong effect on the child, and when nature becomes silent, the evenings darker, and life must be lived indoors, then an activity with a special focus is called for. The seasons and their festivals have been the educators of man's soul from the earliest times.

When summer with its abundance of sense impressions and activities passes, there comes the desire for inner activity and the wish to transform the gifts of nature. Corn dollies were made for the hungry birds, garlands for the cattle, holly and mistletoe placed over the cowshed door as well as in the home, reminding of the miracle of the Holy Night when cattle kneel in their stalls in homage to the holy birth . . . How children must long to glimpse this miracle!

Today ready-made symbols of Christmas and Advent are mass produced. By creating things together in the family, real wonder, joy, and expectancy are awakened, and the activities and suggestions in this book are for parents who wish to foster such feelings in their children.

When Christmas Day arrives, the telling of the birth story from Luke's Gospel and the setting of the crib scene with the shepherds can be the centre of the family circle. Later, after New Year, the account from Matthew's Gospel of the coming of the kings and their arrival on January 6 can be told, and this group placed under the tree.

This book aims to help children and parents find meaning and feel reverence in the preparation for this great festival of the year.

Audrey McAllen

Advent calendar

This simple Advent calendar can easily be made by children in the lower school classes, and even by their younger brothers and sisters. With their own hands they make the Christmas star and see it gradually draw near. Later this experience can be taken up into their thinking.

Materials:
1 Sheet of A3 (16½″ × 11¾″) cartridge paper
1 Sheet of A5 (8¼″ × 6″) cartridge paper (thick enough to stand)

Cut a double door at the bottom of the larger sheet. To keep the doors closed stick a paper flap on to one of the doors. On the other door stick a keeper. The keeper should only be stuck down at the ends so that the flap can be pushed through.

The Christmas picture — Joseph, Mary and the crib — painted on white cartridge paper is stuck behind the door opening.

Above the door make 28 slots* one above the other at equal intervals for the Christmas star. Every day the star comes down one slot until it reaches the crib.

Cut the Christmas star out of

---

* To take account of the longest possible Advent period, 28 slots are necessary.

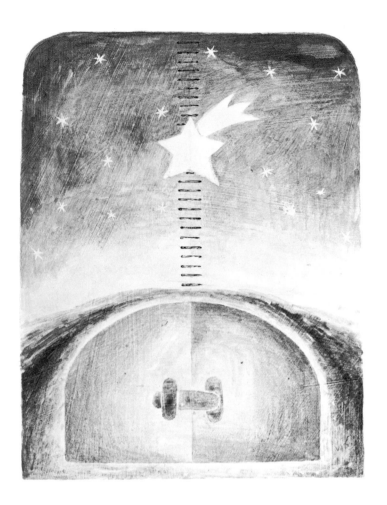

cartridge paper and fix a small tongue on the back to fit into the slot.

On the whole of the front of the calendar paint the grotto, sky and stars.

Advent walnut-chain

The walnut has a special connection to our thinking. We call a difficult problem to solve a 'hard nut to crack'. If we manage to crack the nut we are rewarded with new insight. During Advent we can join several nuts with a band. One nut only is to be cracked each day. This picture symbolizes that much toil and joy are needed before we can meet the greatest mystery of Christmas time.

Materials:
As many walnuts as the days of
  Advent for the year in question
Gold paint
3 to 4 metres (yards) of red ribbon
  2 cm (¾") wide
Filling for the walnuts

Open the nuts with a knife and take out the kernels. Take care not to get the halves that belong to each other mixed up.

Paint the outsides with gold paint; leave to dry. Fill the half nuts. With a touch of adhesive stick the two halves together with the ribbon running between.

Suggestions for contents: A little bell, a dwarf, a shell, a little sheep or rabbit made of teased sheep's wool, a shepherd, a standing doll,* a cradle with child, crystals, a candle, beeswax for modelling, a glass marble, a gold-foil star, a sailing boat (stick a piece of beeswax on to the bottom of half a nutshell and put half a match-stick with a sail into the beeswax), a feather.

Each day one nut is cut off by a different member of the family (or a different child from the class) and so the contents of the nut can be worked out beforehand.

* See the author's *Making Soft Toys*, p.21.

Advent calendar with little parcels

The little parcels, which may be hung by a string, contain crib figures and everything needed for building up a crib (tableau): special stones, straw for the floor of the crib, various cones, beech-nut husks, fruit of the alder, birch-bark, snail-shells. The order can be: first, things from nature, then shepherds and sheep, and finally Mary, Joseph and the Child.

Advent calendar building up a crib
An idea for the whole family

We can use the idea of the Advent calendar to build up a crib in sequence. On each Advent Sunday things from one of the kingdoms of nature are collected.

On the first of Advent begin by arranging the most beautiful stones found by each person around the place for the crib.

On the second Sunday various mosses, little fir-trees, pot-plants and other plants, even though they are not blossoming, and little bunches of dried flowers are collected.

On the third of Advent bring various animals into the landscape and build the stall.

On the fourth of Advent Mary and Joseph begin to move through the landscape and each day come a step nearer the stall where on Christmas Eve the Child appears.

Table-lantern

This simple little lantern can be painted and stuck together by quite young children. With a wire handle and a stick (and even using a larger cheese box) it is suitable for a Martinmas lantern procession.

Materials:
One small round Swiss cheese box, diameter about 10 cm (4″)
One sheet of drawing paper (not too thick) about 12 cm (5″) high and long enough to go round the cheese box
Water-colours and paint-brushes
Cooking oil
Paper adhesive
One small candle
Aluminium foil

Moisten the drawing-paper and span it smoothly with a sponge on to a board or oil cloth cover.

Paint on the water-colours in wide generous patches. Allow to dry.

Carefully oil the painted paper on both sides with a cloth. Allow to dry fully.

Cut the sides (which are usually high) of the cheese box in half; take the disc out at the top of the box.

Apply glue to both outside edges of the cheese box and to the inner edges of the paper and allow to become tacky.

First stick the paper on to the bottom half and then on to the top half of the cheese box and finally stick the paper together at the joint.

Wind a strip of foil about 3 cm (1″) wide folded over several times round the bottom of the candle. From below cut up to half way. Bend the 'rays' outwards and stick into the base of the lantern with Uhu or similar adhesive. The candle will burn better if some holes are made near the base of the lantern.

Advent clock

by Anke-Usche Clausen

This Advent clock lends a particular charm to the days and weeks of Advent. Instead of pointing to single symbols with its hands, each day it opens up a little bit more until finally a complete picture stands revealed.

It is not easy to make the clock, and careful work and patience are required. With their parents' help even twelve-year-olds might have a try.

Materials:
One sheet stiff drawing-paper 30 × 30 cm (12″ × 12″)
One sheet stiff cartridge paper, same size
Two sheets stiff smooth cardboard, same size
One paper fastener (as used for closing padded envelopes)

On the drawing-paper draw a circle, radius 12.5 cm (5″). Leave a segment about a sixth of the circle free at the bottom. Divide the remainder of the circle into 27 segments (11° each).

Now paint in the whole area of the circle in such a way that as you go round from segment to segment something new can be seen, even though the rest of the picture

remains hidden. In the reserved part below, the Christmas picture is painted.

Along the left hand edge of this part cut a slit from the outside to the centre of the circle. Stick a stiff card behind the centre to strengthen the hole which must be large enough for the paper-fastener to be able to turn easily (see Figure A).

Cut a disc radius 13 cm (5¼″) out of the cardboard. Cut a slit in the disc (as in Figure B) with a spiral round the centre hole which takes the paper fastener. (It is important to make a proper spiral in such a way that there is enough space left between the beginning and the end of the spiral otherwise the disc will break at that point.) In the middle punch a hole for

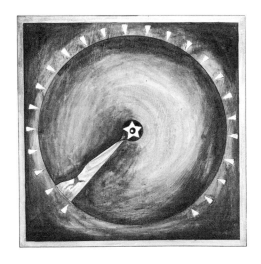

the paper fastener. Stick strengthening behind the spiral and the hole.

Stick a tongue on the left edge of the cut. You hold the tongue when turning the disc.

Fix the disc on to the clock face by means of a paper fastener. As the clock moves round, the disc gradually disappears behind the clock face.

Stick the picture on to the cartridge paper by the corners; the inner part, that is, the clock face behind which the disc disappears, remaining unstuck.

Out of the second sheet of cardboard cut out a hole radius 12.5 cm (5″) and lay the square sheet on to the clock. Stick the edges together with adhesive tape.

Stick on the 28 pointers made of gold paper. Fix a cord at the back for hanging up.

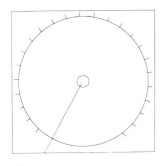

A

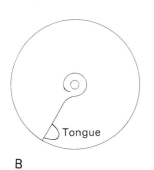

B

Five-pointed-star lantern

Schoolchildren and parents who love geometry and accurate work will find a particular attraction in making the five-pointed-star lantern. The five-pointed stars appear as one works. The five-pointed star is a symbol of life taking on form.

How lovely the lantern light can be on early winter evenings when children gather in a circle for a story.

Materials:
Drawing paper, lampshade paper or parchment
1 Nightlight
Pair of compasses, protractor, ruler, adhesive

Cut out ten pentagons, marking the centre of each side. Recommended length of each side 6 cm (2½"). Angle 108°. On each pentagon score lightly the lines joining the centre points of each side. Fold the corners over to make a flap. Now stick the pentagons together so that each flap projects into the neighbouring pentagon. In this way a five-pointed star appears on every surface. Five surfaces together form the top half and five the bottom of the lantern. At the top and bottom the corners are simply stuck inside. Without a base the light can be more easily lit.

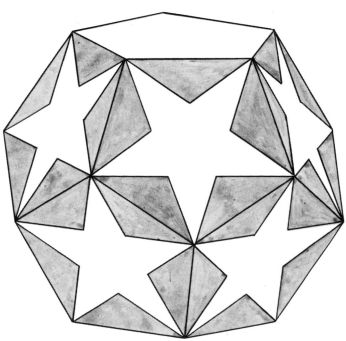

Candle dipping

Candle dipping is a favourite activity for Advent. It is an absorbing experience to see a new candle slowly emerging from the remains of bits of wax which have been carefully collected and melted down. And when the scent of beeswax fills the room and layer by layer a clean new candle gradually takes shape from the liquid, then the idea of renewal is truly experienced. The old year gives up its remains so that the first festival of the young, Christian year may receive its light.

Materials:
Beeswax and other stubs of candles
Thick cotton tow for wicks (or
   candle-wick)
Tall narrow tins
Pot or saucepan for water

Care must be taken with the hot wax and saucepans.
   Put the wax pieces into the tins and

melt in a saucepan of hot water. Dip the wick in for a moment, draw out, allow to cool and smoothe it straight. Keep on dipping in, drawing out and allowing to cool until the desired thickness has been attained. From time to time take a knife and cut off the point of wax that accumulates at the bottom. Keep adding wax to the melting pot. It is a good idea to have a second tin ready with melted wax and to keep on pouring some of this wax into the other tin which is being used for the dipping, so as to keep the level constant.

Where possible allow the finished candle to cool off by hanging, because when left lying it can lose its shape.

Candlesticks can be made of clay or carved out of wood or bark. Never leave candles burning unattended!

Little crib garden

Younger children, older children and parents like making these little crib gardens. We can put so many lovely things from nature — in spite of it being wintertime — into the garden, that the arranging is a real pleasure, and nature's wonders — a pebble or a snail's shell — fill us again and again with amazement. Moreover there is awakened the feeling for the careful preparation that is necessary and that all the kingdoms of nature must be brought in before the Child can appear in the manger. The German writer Novalis once expressed this idea:

> He is the star, he is the sun,
> He is the well of life eternal,
> From plant and stone
>   and sea and light
> Shines forth his childlike
>   countenance.

Little children, when they see their parents or older brothers and sisters building the garden, often want to make one of their own. Every day they change and add something so that the garden becomes more and more complete as Christmas approaches.

Materials:

Discs from tree trunks or branches
    with bark diameter about 15 cm
    (6″), 2 cm (¾″) thick
Flowerpot filled with earth or moss
Fir twigs, rose-hip stalks
Beeswax for modelling and such like

Carve or sandpaper the edges of the disc of a tree-trunk or branch. Sandpaper the surface smooth and apply beeswax or linseed varnish.

Bore five or six holes 4 mm (³/₁₆″) diameter in a semicircle near the edge of the disc to take the various twigs.

Make as many figures as you wish and put them in the garden.

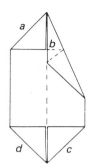

Folded stars made of tissue-paper

Materials:

Tissue-paper

Transparent self-adhesive film

Cut out eight rectangles of the same size, for instance of sides 4 × 8 cm (1½″ × 3″). Fold each rectangle to make one of the points of the star in the following way: Fold the rectangle in half lengthwise and unfold again. Fold over the four corners to the centre-crease so that at each end a point is formed.

Now fold the new sides a, b, c, d, also to the centre.

Repeat with all eight rectangles. These are now the points of the star.

Carefully assemble the eight points on to a piece of transparent self-adhesive film to make the star.

Allow the film to project about 1 cm (½″) beyond the point so that the star can be stuck to the window.

By altering the ratio of the sides of the rectangles and increasing the number of points many variations of the star can be produced.

A star from a knot of transparent paper

It is startling to discover that concealed in every simple knot lies the most ancient and holy mystery of the pentagon and pentagram. The five-pointed star that underlies every rose-blossom was always the symbol of the incarnated human form. The Angel of the Annunciation approaches with the lily-flower which indicates in the six-pointed-star the interpenetration of the heavenly and the earthly triangles. But Mary with the new-born child on her arm sits in the rose garden. Some Christmas carols indicate this (for instance, 'A rose has come to blossom . . .').

Make a knot in a strip of paper of any width. As you press the knot flat make sure that the corners are well pointed. Cut off one end of the strip along the edge of the pentagon. Fold the other end to the back, cut off in the same way and stick on lightly.

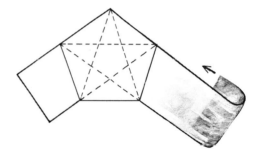

Star made of gold foil

Materials:
Gold coloured aluminium foil
  (paper-backed)
Uhu or other glue

On a piece of paper draw a circle, radius 5 cm (2″), and with the same radius mark off the six points of a hexagon round the circumference. Mark the mid point of each side and connect it to the centre. Draw a smaller circle, radius about 2 cm (¾″) and mark a smaller hexagon on it, using the lines crossing this circle, so that it is staggered against the larger.

Now connect these points to the outer points to make the arms of the star. Draw only five arms.

Prick the points of the figure through onto the gold foil with a needle or the point of a pair of compasses, and with a hard, sharp pencil and ruler draw the star.

Cut out the arms of the star. Crease each arm along its base.

Cut into the centre from one side of the missing arm. Fold this flap and stick it under the neighbouring one. There will now be a little five-sided pyramid at the centre of the star.

A thin thread can be stuck to the centre to hang the star. Two stars can be stuck back to back: point to point, or staggered.

5 cm (2″)

A straw star

This requires some patience and skill.

Materials:
Thirty straws of the same length,
    ironed flat and cut to a point
    (the best length to start with is
    10 cm, 4")
Adhesive

Stick a star together out of five straws. Take care to weave each straw over and under as in the drawing. Stick the straws together lightly at the points.

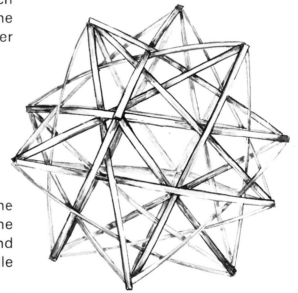

Build a second star on to one of the straws of the first star on the same principle. One point of the second star will now project into the middle of the first star.

Go on building star by star until all thirty straws have been used, seeing that at every point five stars meet and thus six five-pointed stars are interlocked.

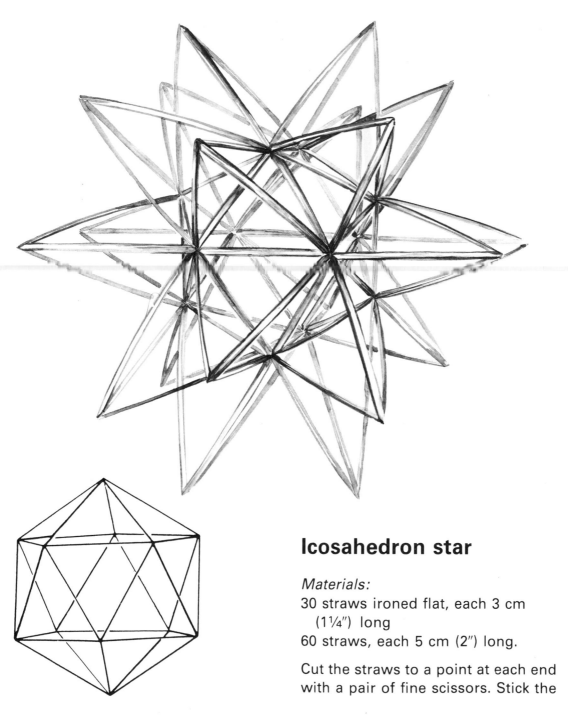

Icosahedron star

Materials:
30 straws ironed flat, each 3 cm
   (1¼") long
60 straws, each 5 cm (2") long.

Cut the straws to a point at each end
with a pair of fine scissors. Stick the

thirty short straws together to make an icosahedron; that is, stick ten triangles together to form a belt. Then stick five triangles on top of the belt to form a point, and five triangles in the same way at the bottom. Over each triangle stick three of the longer straws to form a star point.

The shepherds' crib

Materials:
Coloured scraps of material and felt
Scraps of fur
Pink tricot
Brown and white unspun sheep's
  wool
Unspun Shetland wool and camel-
  hair

Mary, Joseph and the Shepherds
Twist some finely teased sheep's wool into a thick roll and tie a thread at one end to form a head.

Make a fairly tight dress without sleeves out of quite thick cloth or felt. Pull it over the roll of wool so that the figure will stand.

Cut *Mary's* cloak out of a rectangular piece of blue cloth or felt and fasten it round her head and shoulders with a few stitches. Sew the hands into the folds of the cloak.

The head and hands can be covered with tricot. Touch in the eyes and mouth with a coloured pencil.*

* See the author's *Making Soft Toys*, p.21.

25

Joseph and the shepherds have a cloak of cloth or fur laid over their shoulders. Fasten at the neck back and front with a few stitches. You can put a staff inside. The hair is made of finely teased brown sheep's wool which is fixed on together with the hat. Make the hat out of a round piece of felt. The middle of the hat is rounded by drawing a crimp thread through. Sew on to the head with a few stitches.

The Child

The child has swaddling clothes and a band made of light coloured cloth or felt.

The sheep

The sheep can be made out of a piece of fur cut into a rectangle. Roll together around the short edges and sew together underneath and at the ends with a leather-needle. Tie off about one third to make the head. Now clip the sheep so that it gets its proper shape. Sew on ears of soft leather or felt.

Ox and ass

There are several ways of making the ox and ass:

1. Fold the two ends of a hank of well carded unspun Shetland wool inwards, and using a few stitches with a fine thread model a lying ass. Form the ears by gently drawing out the wool. For the ox take camel-hair or light brown combed sheepswool.

2. With pipe-cleaners the animals' shape can be formed. Wind unspun grey or brown wool on to the wire,

The stable

The stable can be made from short pieces of wood which still have the bark on them and the roof from pieces of bark or thin 'backs'. Furnishing the crib with straw, moss, plants, stones, and so on gives plenty of scope for good ideas.

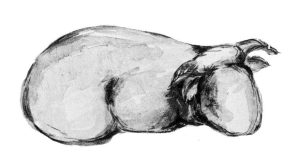

The kings' crib

In order to make a clear distinction between the two sets of crib figures, we recommend that instead of felt you should use some soft flowing material for the Mary in this crib. She has a golden head-band. According to ancient tradition she has the Child on her lap.

Whereas the shepherds' Joseph had a brown cloak, now the kings' Joseph should have a mantle of brown and violet material.

Materials:
Unspun sheep's wool (white, brown, black)
Pipe-cleaners
White material for the mantles
Gold coloured aluminium foil (two-sided)
Wooden blocks (pieces cut from a broomstick)

Make the heads out of sheep's wool and cover with pale pink tricot. Touch in the eyes and mouth with a coloured pencil. Cover the hands also with tricot.

You can take a wooden block for the *Kings* and the *Angel*, and nail or staple on to it the upper part of the figure made of wire. The ends of the wire are pushed into the head which

is covered with tricot. Wind some sheepswool thickly round the upper part of the body and not so thickly round the arms. This ensures that the figures will stand firmly and they can be clothed in loosely falling

garments. The arms of the kings can be bent to carry their gifts, and those of the angel to hold the star-stave.

Make the *garments* out of white material. Make a red, green and blue stole for the kings. The angel has a golden band crossed over the breast, and a girdle.

Only now can the hair and beards of finely shredded sheep's wool be sewn on:

Blue king: white
Red king: brown
Green king: black

The kings have toothed crowns made of gold foil, and the angel has a golden circlet with a star.

Transparencies

by Anke-Usche Clausen

These transparencies have evolved out of teaching children for many years. Every year the younger pupils do simple designs in colour while the older ones make large window compositions.

A rich variety of colour tones can be achieved with this kind of transparency consisting of slightly crinkled tissue-paper laid in loose layers between two white transparent sheets. The colours are not defined by sharp contours, but are seen in a diversity of interplay and transition, thus creating the living ambience for the figures.

If in the composition of a picture the colours are used according to their inner nature, then the forms and perspectives come alive (for instance, red, the active colour, springs towards the viewer, while blue draws him into the distance). In a wood for example, the nearer trees will have a reddish hue while the trees in the background will have a bluish and darker tinge. In this way depth of space is achieved in colour.

As the position of the viewer changes, or as the source of light moves in the course of the day new shades of colour appear in the inter-

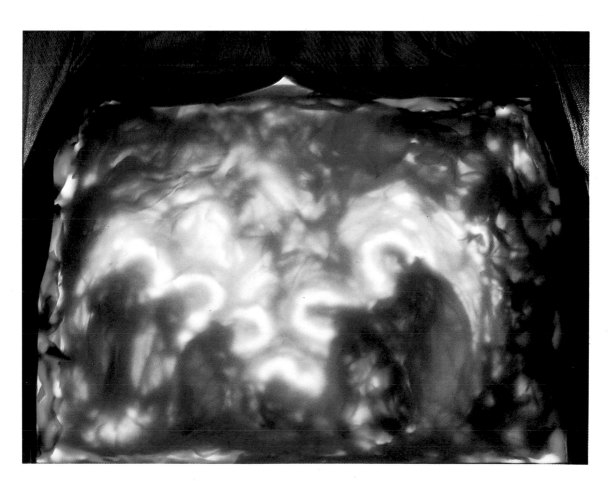

vening spaces, altering the mood of the whole. And as you look upon the picture for some time, not only are your sense of colour and your powers of imagination stimulated, but also a sense of tranquillity arises, for now the deeper layers of consciousness have been affected.

By using plant-dyed sheepswool or silk veils this technique can be developed further. (This is particularly recommended for puppet-show scenery.) Equally suitable are pictures painted on transparent paper with wax colours. For painting we recommend a pane of glass warmed by a lamp below.

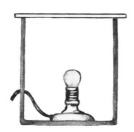

As a background while making the transparency stick a sheet of white transparent paper at the corners to a window pane, or stand a pane at a slant in front of an electric light, or put the lamp in a ventilated box with the pane over the top.

Materials:
2 sheets white transparent paper
  (tracing-paper)
Tissue-paper in many colours:
  where possible obtain the
  primary colours (yellow, red, blue)
  in several shades
  (Missing shades can be made by
  using water-colours and a soft
  sponge)
Gold cardboard for the frame
Adhesive

There is no scissor-cutting in this kind of transparency. The sheets of tissue-paper are not laid flat on top of each other, but are modelled. Tear off (do not cut) a piece of paper of the desired size, crush it into a ball and smoothe it out again, then crinkling it push it together (do not fold) and stick it here and there to the background. The paper pushed thus together in waves remains translucent and so the differentiation of colours is effected. Further gradations are achieved by layering one colour surface over the other. If you intend to make people or animals, first lay out the general idea of the transparency leaving room for the individual figures. Then each figure must harmonize and be taken up into the general colour surroundings. In some places the figure may need a transition of colour, in others it will contrast sharply with another colour.

When making a human or an animal figure start by tearing off a piece of paper which is longer and wider than the final size of the figure — this allows for the crinkling. Two or more perfectly overlapping layers of tissue-paper give a fuller colour strength.

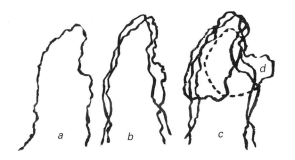

It is not difficult to make human figures merge into their surroundings. Take for example a shepherd. Tear off the clothing for the whole figure, crush it, push it together a little and stick loosely to the background. Then tear a smaller narrower piece; stick it loosely on to the first piece so that it does not quite cover it. A third even smaller piece makes the deepening of the colour towards the back (like a cloak). For the head tear off a round or oblong piece of light pink tissue-paper. Apply a little adhesive and as you stick it on, draw the paper together in a few places under the nose and round the mouth. In this way you will strengthen the pink colour tones in those places and the figure takes on

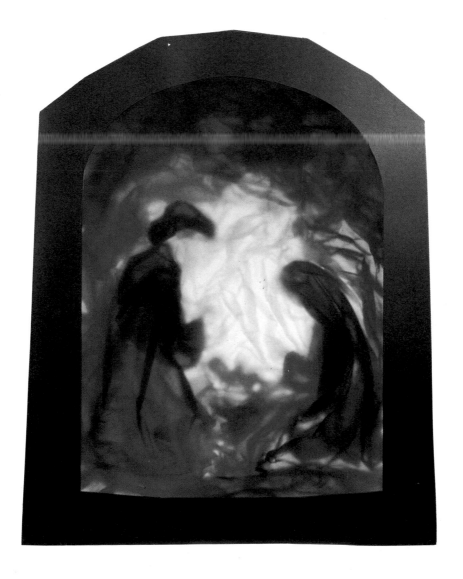

36

a facial expression. For hair tear off a piece of tracing-paper of a different colour (reddish, yellowish, light blue, ultramarine and so on), crush, and stick on in a few places. The shepherds' hats and capes are made in the same way (push a kind of fold in from the top down to the bottom edge: in this way the hat is strengthened along the brim). Do not stick the arms on like thin sausages but insert them as strips of varying width between the first and second layer and allow them to peep out a bit. Let the paper form waves as you stick it on.

When the picture is finished stick it on to a frame (from behind). Depending on the size of the transparency make the frame of wood or corrugated cardboard 5 to 20 mm (¼" to ¾") thick. Cover the front of the picture with the second sheet of transparent paper. After fixing one side, fix the opposite side before moving round.

If gold cardboard is to be used for the frame, cut out a window to the desired shape and stick on the second sheet of transparent paper behind. Stick on a little roll of paper 5 to 20 mm (¼" to ¾") thick behind the window-frame all the way round, and paste the finished transparency on to this.

More transparencies

For many years Gerda Funhoff has been developing a technique of cutting out coloured tissue-paper and has produced a large number of motifs from which the following transparencies are a selection. By following the instructions carefully you can quickly master the technique, and as your experience increases you can develope your own designs.

Using the same methods with paper Gerda Funhoff has set up a large fairy-tale stage for coloured shadow puppet-shows.

Materials:

Coloured tissue-paper or similar stronger paper (the following colours being particularly recommended: light and dark yellow, carmine red, three shades of blue, two shades of purple, pink, green
Gold cardboard (at least 6-sheet)
Non-dripping glue

Instruments:

Pair of small sharp scissors
Pair of compasses
Stanley knife for cutting cardboard (particularly for the window-frames)

1. Mary with stars

Frame size:
about 17 × 25 cm (7″ × 10″)
Background:
1 double sheet of dark yellow paper
2 double sheets of light yellow paper

Lay the dark yellow double sheet inside one of the two light yellow double sheets.

Set the compasses to a radius of approx 6 cm (2½″). Place the point about 2 cm (¾″) below the bottom edge of the paper and draw an arc. Reducing the radius successively by 7 mm (¼″) draw three further arcs.

Cut the smallest segment out of all four layers. Cut the arc above out of the three top layers, the next out of two and the last out of the top layer only so that you have four gradations of colour.

About 8 cm (3″) from the top edge,

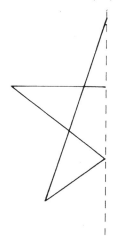

and offset a little to the left of the centre line, draw a circle with a radius of about 3 cm (1¼"). Draw in the background for the figure of Mary and cut both out of all four layers.

Mark the stars and cut out of all four layers by folding.

Disregarding the stars cut out the upper part of the background for Mary first out of the second top layer and then slightly more from the top layer.

Lay all these sheets inside the second light yellow double sheet. This is the sheet on which the figure of Mary will be built up.

First fold Mary's cloak in such a way that the head is inclined forward and fits into the lightest background, and the back and the hem-line just cover the edges of light background by a few millimetres.

Cut out the red robe, face and hand for Mary and stick them on to the cloak.

Now stick the whole figure (Mary) on to the background but only at the robe and face.

Cut away the yellow background under Mary's cloak leaving only a tiny edge for sticking.

Stick Mary's cloak to the edges and stick white tissue-paper on behind.

Cut out the frame out of gold cardboard.

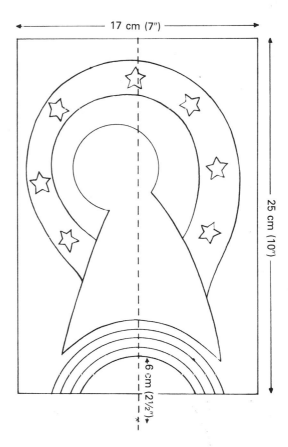

Stick the transparency on to the back of the frame and carefully stick the single layers together by the outer edges on top of each other.

Score lightly along the outer edge of the frame on the gold side, then the flaps can be bent backwards easily.

2. Advent boat

Frame size:
about 12 × 22 cm (4¾″ × 8¾″)
Background:
1 double sheet dark yellow paper
2 double sheets light yellow paper,
size about 12 × 11 cm
(4¾″ × 4¼″) for the top half of the
transparency. For the bottom half
use various blue and purple
sheets

Lay the dark yellow double sheet
inside one of the light yellow double
sheets. Fold over lightly to make a
faint vertical centre line.

Set the compass at a radius of
approximately 15 mm (⅝″). Place the
point of the compass on the centre
line about 55 mm (2⅛″) below the
top edge, and draw a circle. Increasing the radius each time by about 6
mm (¼″) draw three more circles.

Using a fold, cut the smallest circle
out of all the layers, the next circle
out of the top three, and so on; so
as to create a sun which becomes
brighter and brighter towards the
centre.

Below the sun draw horizontal
wavy lines and cut out in gradation.
On the top layer make high waves,
and on the other layers make the
waves successively lower.

Lay this double sheet (which has

been worked on) inside the second double sheet and cut off the latter in a wavy line a bit below the last horizontal wavy line.

Fold the child's garment in such a way that the folds run to a point at the neck and fan out towards the bottom, the finished length being about 5 cm (2") of red paper. If necessary clip the shoulders in a bit.

Cut the hair out of two light yellow layers which do not quite fit over each other. Cut the face and hands out of double pink paper (two sheets stuck together).

Stick on the child so that its head,

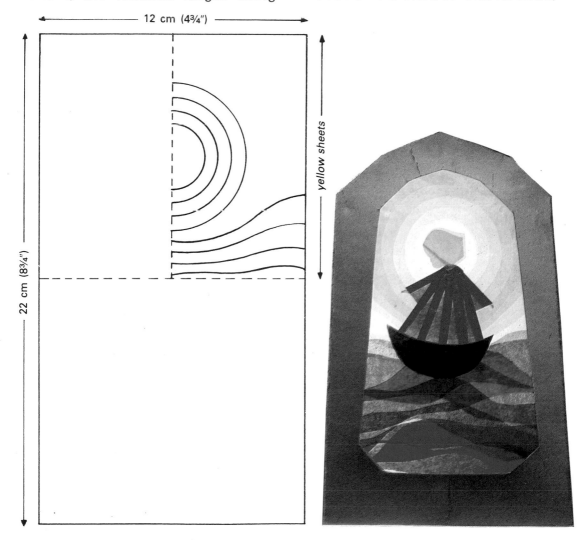

slightly bent, is in the middle of the sun. Cut the little boat out of three layers of dark purple paper stuck together, and stick on to the background.

Cut the waves out of strips of paper which span the whole width of the transparency, the top and bottom edges of the strip being wavy. Begin with the light blue and stick on so that it slightly overlaps the yellow. Cut each wave layer differently and stick either in front or behind. Use dark blue and purple shades towards the bottom. About seven wave layers are needed in all.

Finish the frame as for Mary with the stars.

3. Mary and Joseph by the crib

Frame size:
about 35 × 25 cm (14″ × 10″)
Background
1 double sheet of dark yellow paper
2 double sheets light yellow paper
1 single sheet of light yellow paper

Lay the dark yellow double sheet inside one of the light yellow double sheets, with the folded edge at the top of the picture.

About 3 cm (1¼″) from the top cut out a star (using the folding cut) from all four layers. Now drop the bottom layer and cut out a slightly larger similar star from the remaining

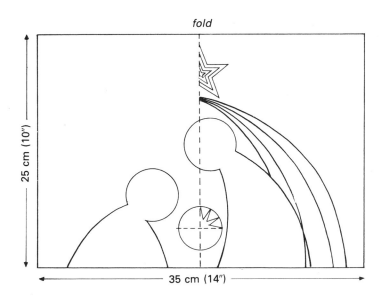

fold

25 cm (10″)

35 cm (14″)

layers. Continue layer by layer increasing the size of the star.

From the uppermost layers cut out symmetrically (by folding) the first background arch, then increase the size of the arches each time in the consecutive layers.

Draw the halos and light surroundings for Mary, Joseph and the crib, but cut out only round the crib.

Stick the single sheet of light yellow paper on behind at the top edge only.

Cut out (by folding) about four rays from the upper half of the halo round the crib.

Now cut out the light surroundings of Mary and Joseph from the two bottom layers (disregarding the arches).

Lay all these prepared layers inside the second light yellow double sheet.

Cut out the crib from the three-layered dark purple paper (stuck together) and stick on.

Cut out the Child from the three-layered pink paper (stuck together) and stick on.

Fold Mary's cloak and on to it stick her face, robe and hand.

Stick on the figure of Mary only at the sides here and there. Cut away the yellow background underneath the blue cloak leaving only a narrow edge for sticking. Stick on a white sheet at the back.

Fold Joseph's cloak and stick on, likewise hat, face, beard and hand. Cut away the staff behind the cloak and hand.

Cut out the frame from gold-card and stick the transparency on behind.

4. Little Mary

Frame size: about 10 × 10 cm
   (4″ × 4″)
Background:
1 double sheet light yellow paper
2 double sheets light yellow paper
   size about 11 × 11 cm (4¼″ ×
   4¼″) (The discarded corners of
   the crib transparency can be
   used)

Lay the dark yellow double sheet inside the light yellow double sheet. Cut off the right-hand bottom corner in a gentle arc.

Set the compass radius to about 1 cm (⅜″) and draw a circle touching the arc. Keeping the same centre but increasing the radius each time by about 5 mm (3/16″) draw three further circles cutting the original arc. Cut out the smallest circle from all four layers, the next largest from the three top layers and so on.

Lay the four layers inside the second light yellow double sheet.

Mary's cloak consists of five different layers:

1. Cut the whole cloak out of lighter blue.
2. Cut the whole cloak out of mid-blue. Cut in about three folds which come to a point at the top, and stick on to the first layer.
3. From mid-blue cut a head-dress to the shape of the cloak, but leaving the lap uncovered. Cut folds as in second layer and stick on to the two layers.
4. Cut a second head-dress from mid-blue, but shorter this time and without folds.
5. Cut a further complete cloak from mid-blue and stick on top.

Cut out Mary's robe (red), the child and Mary's face (pink), and stick on in front of the cloak.

Cut out the frame of gold cardboard.

Stick Mary and the sun-background together at the edges only, in such a way that the child is in the innermost sun, and yet all kept within the frame.

Cut away the yellow layers behind Mary's cloak except for a narrow edge and stick a white sheet of transparent paper on to the back.

Stick into the frame.

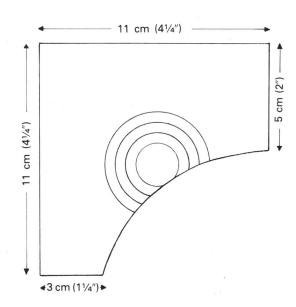

11 cm (4¼")
11 cm (4¼")
5 cm (2")
3 cm (1¼")

Celebrating Advent in the southern hemisphere

by Audrey McAllen

In the southern hemisphere the date of the Christmas celebration falls at the summer solstice when the midsummer experience is what the child is living in, and stimulation of a northern-hemisphere mood would be disrupting.

A midsummer mood and activity should precede the day when we celebrate this unique birthday, For instance, a crown of roses can be made, thus gathering the fruits of summer in an image of pure love found in the cradle of the nativity.

The observation of what nature is providing can be the guideline for activity, and pictures of the Madonna in nature would seem to be especially suitable for the situation in the southern hemisphere, (for example, the Botticelli, where a praying Madonna kneels before the sleeping babe who is lying beside a rose bush, or Dürer's white-clad Madonna in a garden with animals). At the summer solstice on December 22 the story of Zachariah and John the Baptist's birth could be told so that a feeling for the culmination of the year and a turning point in time is marked.

For the actual winter solstice in June, a kind of 'Advent time' could certainly be made in connection with the four kingdoms of nature which could provide motifs for transparencies. This can also be a time for making candles and stars, reflecting the warmth and love in our hearts in winter time. These reflect the inner love in our hearts, being the underlying mood which the adult needs to prepare this drawing together of the family circle at the time when the sun is away in the northern hemisphere.

A custom from the north valid in both parts of the earth is the recording of the weather for the twelve days of Christmas. Older children could record the daily weather and compare this with the weather during the following twelve months, one day being equivalent to a month. A story or verse for the twelve nights could be read or an Advent-type calendar made where behind each door is one of the zodiac constellations or symbols through which the sun passes in his yearly journey from hemisphere to hemisphere.

Freya Jaffke

Making Soft Toys

This book tells how to make simple children's toys (puppets, dolls, and special surprises) with very little cost and using only natural materials. Through detailed but simple instructions and sketches, the reader will easily progress to the creation of original toys from materials at hand.

In an era of mechanical toys and television, this book helps to satisfy the young child's great need for unsophisticated toys which cultivate the imagination.

Gisela Bittleston

The Healing Art of
Glove Puppetry

This book describes all the basic aspects of glove puppetry. It tells you how to make puppets and let them act, how to construct a puppet theatre with lighting and other additions, how to put on a performance and write your own scripts. There follow four fairy-tale plays, and the author concludes the book with a note on the meaning of these fairy tales.

Alice A Gorge

Creative Toymaking
Dolls Animals Puppets

The child is living in a world quite different from ours, and we have to understand this if a toy is really to give the right kind of satisfaction. The child is not interested in naturalistic detail and exact imitation. He therefore asks for simple toys of bright, harmoniously combined colours that will speak in a living way to his mind and heart.

In this book Alice Gorge explains how children and adults can make all kinds of colourful toys from cotton, corduroy, dishcloths, dusters, felt, rayon, towelling and wool. The toys described include wool and felt balls; cushion, tied and knotted dolls; chicks, ducks, hens, horses, donkeys and an elephant; glove, handkerchief and knotted puppets, and many more.

But this book goes further than just describing how to make soft toys. It shows how the making of soft toys can be a creative activity which, as you practice it, can become an art, or at least can release unsuspected artistic abilities, and can be a means of satisfying self-expression.

Floris Books